Planes
and Helicopters

Written by
Sally Hewitt and Nicola Wright

Designed by
Chris Leishman

Illustrated by
Rachael O'Neill

Contents

Watts

LONDON · NEW YORK · SYDNEY

Flying

Planes can fly because they have engines and wings. Engines push the plane along the runway. Air rushes over the wings and lifts the plane into the air.

Flyer Fun Fact

In 1903 Orville Wright made the first controlled flight in history. It lasted for only 12 seconds!

Cockpit

Tail

Turbo fan engines

Fuselage (body)

Wings

Undercarriage (landing wheels)

Helicopters do not need runways. Their engines drive rotors that spin and lift the helicopter straight up into the air.

Main rotor

Tail

Tail rotor

Cockpit

Skids

Engines
Propellers
Some planes have propellers. The engines make the propellers spin round on the front of the plane.

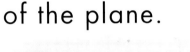

Jets The fastest planes have jet engines. Jet engines suck in air and push it out behind them.

In the cockpit

The pilot controls the plane from the cockpit. In airliners this is usually called the flight deck. Lots of screens and dials give the pilots all the information they need to fly the plane.

Microphone

Runway

Pilot (Captain)

Earphones

Co-pilot

Special instruments

Control stick

The pilot moves the control stick backwards, forwards and sideways to control the plane.

Autopilot This is a computer that controls a plane in flight. Pilots control the take-off, but the autopilot can do most of the work during the flight, and even land the plane!

Airliners

Each year, millions of passengers are carried all over the world in airliners. The largest are jumbo jets that carry more than 500 passengers. Small airliners carry 20 to 30 people.

Cabin

Upper deck

Flight deck

British Aerospace Jetstream

Passengers

DC9

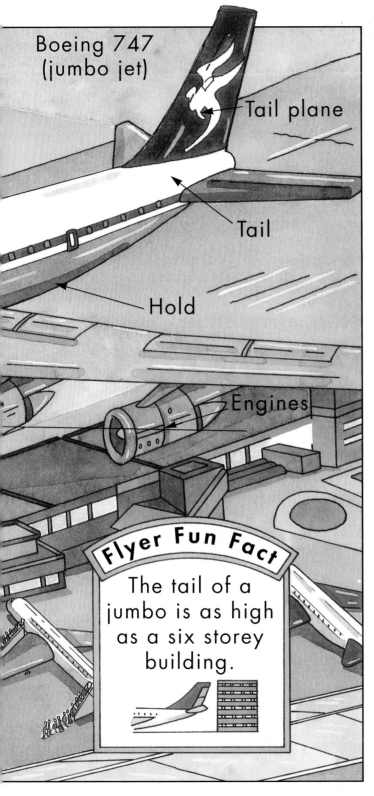

Boeing 747
(jumbo jet)

Tail plane

Tail

Hold

Engines

Flyer Fun Fact

The tail of a
jumbo is as high
as a six storey
building.

Airliner shapes

Four engines Some airliners have four engines, two on each wing.

Three engines Some have three engines, one on each wing and one on the tail.

Two engines Some have two engines, on the wings or on either side of the tail.

Concorde

Concorde is the world's fastest airliner. It is supersonic, which means it flies faster than the speed of sound.

Streamlined shape

Passenger cabin

Delta-shaped win

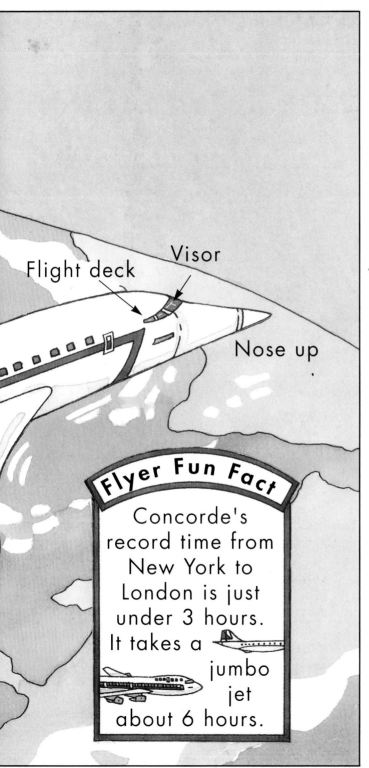

Flight deck

Visor

Nose up

Flyer Fun Fact

Concorde's record time from New York to London is just under 3 hours. It takes a jumbo jet about 6 hours.

Concorde facts

Concorde has four engines and can fly at more than 2,000 km/h.

Its visor and nose can be drooped down to let the pilot see the runway clearly.

When Concorde reaches the speed of sound, you can hear a double bang.

Special planes

Here are some unusual planes from around the world.

The Harrier jump jet can take off straight up into the air like a helicopter. Then it swivels its jet engines round and flies forward.

Floats

Seaplanes have floats instead of wheels. They can land on water.

Jet engines

The Galaxy military plane is huge. It can carry heavy loads of tanks, trucks and soldiers.

Refuelling

Small fighters cannot carry much fuel.

On long flights they refuel from special refuelling planes. The big plane has long pipes coming from its fuel tanks. The small plane fits a probe into a pipe and takes in fuel.

Aerobatics

Pilots control a plane's movement by changing the position of flaps on the tail and wings. Display teams, like these Red Arrows, can roll, loop and spin their planes. This is called aerobatics.

Smoke trails

Single turbofan engine

Flyer Fun Fact

People used to perform in flying circuses by standing on the wings of planes while they flew!

Formation

Controlling

Pitch is the up and down movement. It is controlled by the elevator flaps.

Yaw is sideways movement. It is controlled by the rudder.

Bank or Roll Moving the ailerons on the wings makes a plane roll over.

Turning is done by banking.

Small planes

Small planes can be fun for sport or they can do special kinds of work.

The tiny Pitts Special biplane was built to do extraordinary aerobatics.

Pitts Special

Microlight

Microlights are hang-gliders with engines. They are used for sport.

The bubble-shaped cockpit of the Optica gives pilots a clear view of the ground. It is used by some police forces.

Optica

Piper Aztec

Small propeller planes like this Piper Aztec can carry two to six people.

Around the world

Small planes are used around the world for special jobs.

Landing on ice

Flying doctors

Crop spraying

Gliders

A glider has no engines to power it. An aeroplane, truck or a winch has to tow it along until it is going fast enough to fly on its own.

Light body

Long narrow wings

The pilot releases the winch line when the glider is high in the air.

Winch line

The longest flight made by a glider flying in a straight line is 1,460 km.

Thermals

Streamlined shape

Rising currents of warm air (called thermals) keep the glider in the air.

Hang gliders

The pilot can be launched by being towed by a winch, or by running down a hillside.

The pilot is strapped in beneath the fabric wings. He or she uses a control bar and body movements to steer the glider.

17

Helicopters at work

Helicopters make good working machines because they can land and take off in very small spaces. They can also move up, down, backwards, forwards and sideways, and even hover in one place.

Passenger helicopters fly between airports, or take crew and supplies to oil platforms.

Movements

Up and down When the pilot tilts the rotor blade upwards, the helicopter lifts into the air.

Forwards and backwards Tipping the rotor forwards makes the helicopter fly forwards. When the rotor is tipped back, it flies backwards.

Tipping the rotor sideways makes it fly to the left or the right.

Flyer Fun Fact

The first helicopter flew in 1907. It lifted 1 metre off the ground for about 20 seconds!

Search and rescue

Helicopters are very useful for search and rescue at sea.

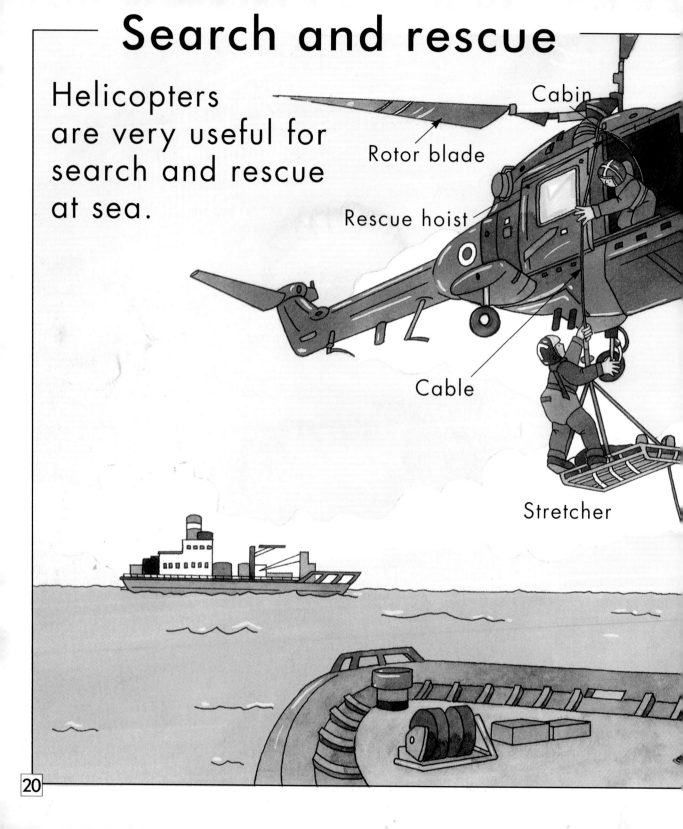

Cabin

Rotor blade

Rescue hoist

Cable

Stretcher

One crew member goes down on a cable and puts a special collar round the person being rescued. Then the cable is winched up into the helicopter with both people attached.

Collar

Skycranes

Big, powerful helicopters are used as skycranes. They can lift and carry heavy loads to places that are very difficult to reach.

Sliding doors

Cargo hook

Main wheels

Flyer Fun Fact

The largest helicopter ever built was the Mil Mi-12. It could lift the weight of nearly 6 elephants!

Tail wheels

Sling load

Special features

The Chinook helicopter has twin rotors that turn in opposite directions.

Safety The big rotors turn safely, high above people's heads.

Some helicopters have an opening in the cabin floor so the crew can watch the load below.

Index

Consultant: Captain Ian Evans
Editors: Nicola Wright & Dee Turner
Design Manager: Kate Buxton
Series concept: Tony Potter
Colour separations: RCS Graphics Ltd, Leeds
Printers: G Canale & Co SpA, Italy

This book was created by Times Four Publishing Ltd, 5 High Street, Cuckfield, Sussex RH17 5EN

First published in 1993 by Watts Books

Copyright ©Times Four Publishing Ltd

A CIP catalogue record for this book is available from the British Library.

Dewey Decimal Classification 629.133

ISBN 0 7496 1026 3 (HB) ISBN 0 7496 3014 0 (PB)

10 9 8 7 6 5 4 3 2 1